Companies Don't Succeed...

PEOPLE DO

The Art of Recognition

By Mac Anderson

Chairman and Founder of Successories, Inc.

Graphics by Balance Design

Treat **Your** **PEOPLE** like your customers

rule # 1

"A successful company can only be built one satisfied customer at a time."

rule # 2

"Rule #1 can only be done with happy, motivated employees."

It is a law of human nature that your employees will never treat customers any better than they are being treated. I'm certain there are many managers who'll disagree and say, "They work here, they get paid and they'll treat customers the way I tell them to treat customers." This theory looks good on paper but it simply doesn't work.

The managers who truly understand this simple premise are the managers of the future. As a leader, they realize that most employees don't care how much you know, until they know how much you care. Therefore, a great deal of their time is spent listening, educating and trying to create the kind of environment that allows people to reach their full potential. They also understand that implementing effective recognition programs to celebrate successes and to thank people for a job well done is crucial to having happy and motivated employees.

"EMPLOYEES will never treat customers any better than they are being treated."

INVEST in your employees

*a*nyone who has experienced the atmosphere at Walt Disney World can attest that Disney is an organization built upon their investment in people as much as anything else. They actually have a seminar which spells out their "Pixie Dust" formula so others can learn from their successful people programs. Unlike many companies, they don't overlook the need to invest in their most valuable asset, their employees.

While the cost of people is one of the largest expenditures for companies, the need to motivate, encourage and recognize them does not receive the attention it should. Retaining employees is becoming more and more difficult. Good people, with the right attitude, who possess the right skills, who hold the knowledge and customer relationships are not easily replaced. The cost of turnover can be substantial. Even more expensive is the disruption and opportunity cost caused by undervalued employees changing jobs.

But so much of this disruption is preventable. A poll of Fortune 1000 companies indicated that "limited recognition and praise" was the number one reason people change jobs. In today's workplace, the investment in programs to acknowledge and congratulate employee effort is money well spent. It's the preventive maintenance that should not be overlooked. Like an oil change for an automobile, it is recognition and praise that will keep the organization moving smoothly, and that will help avoid the expensive, disruptive breakdowns caused by employee turnover.

"Happy employees, not TQM or reengineering hold the KEY to the future productivity and company success." William A. Jenkins

UNDERSTAND
the Psychology
of Recognition

To understand why recognition is important we must understand its role in employee motivation.

First of all, what is motivation? The definition I like is: "An inner drive that compels behavior." The subject has been studied for years, and as far back as Aristotle and Plato, many theories have come forth about why certain people are highly motivated to achieve and others simply don't care. In the simple definition above, the key word is "inner." Motivation is a complex subject because all motivation comes from within, and since we're all different . . . well, need I say more.

Noted psychologist Dr. Abraham Maslow provided the most popular theory on motivation and its impact on human behavior. He wrote that all human beings have a hierarchy of needs that control behavior. Once our physical needs are met (i.e. food, water, shelter) we are only motivated by what he calls our basic human needs. As you can see in Maslow's hierarchy below, recognition, or the desire to feel important in the eyes of others, plays a key role in influencing our behavior at home and in the workplace.

- The Need for Security, *to feel safe.*
- The Need for Recognition, *what I do is important to others.*
- The Need for Acceptance, *what I am is important to others.*
- The Need for New Experiences.

"The human SPIRIT is nurtured by praise, as much as a seedling is nurtured by the soil, the water and the sun." Mario Fernandez

TAP into

HEART

POWER

$a$ccording to Jim Harris, the author of *Getting Employees to Fall in Love With Your Company*, heart power is at the very core of any successful enterprise. Capture the heart, and you have captured the employee. Without a vibrant, beating heart, any business will die. How do you do it? Harris feels (and I totally agree) that three things are crucial:

- Compelling Vision . . . Employees of every company want to know what you stand for and where you're going. It must be an understandable, focused, and wholehearted attempt to arouse passions. Proverbs 29:18 says it best, "Where there is no vision, the people perish."

- Balance Work and Family . . . When companies forget to help their employees balance the demands of work with the need for a personal life, they risk burning out, or losing their best talent. According to Ann McGee-Cooper, author of *You Don't Have to Go Home From Work Exhausted*, the single greatest element of high-energy living is balance; the greater the balance, the greater the joy, energy and creativity.

- Celebrate and Have Fun . . . How can managers expect employees to fall in love with a company that is boring, stoic and staid? Positive fun, genuine appreciation, and the celebration of success will make you want to come to work in the morning.

"The highest achievable level of service comes from the HEART, so the company that reaches peoples' hearts will provide the very best service." Hal Rosenbluth

CLOSE the PERCEPTION GAP

the perception gap that exists between employees and managers on the importance of recognition is astounding. While most managers agree that recognition is a good thing, few realize how passionately their employees feel about the subject.

Bob Nelson, author of *1001 Ways to Reward Employees*, discovered that what managers perceived as most important to employees was sharply different from what the employees actually reported as being most important. Managers and employees were asked to rank 10 items from 1 (most important) to 10 (least important). The results below clearly show that to help employees reach their full potential, managers need to increase their awareness of what motivates employees.

	Managers	Employees
Good Wages	1	5
Job Security	2	4
Promotion/Growth Opportunities	3	7
Good Working Conditions	4	9
Interesting Work	5	6
Personal Loyalty to Workers	6	8
Tactful Disciplining	7	10
Full Appreciation for Work Done	8	1
Sympathetic to Personal Problems	9	3
Feeling "In" On Things	10	2

"You get the best effort from others not by lighting a fire beneath them, but by BUILDING a fire within." Bob Nelson

11

it Starts
AT THE TOP

recognition is about thanking people, listening, and treating people with dignity. If your company has had a reputation for none of the above, then don't expect an insincere recognition program to change anything. The culture of any company starts at the top, and filters down throughout the organization. If you're sitting in that chair, you must ask yourself, "Is employee morale what it should be?" And more importantly, "If not, what can we do to make it better?" Winston Churchill puts it a little more bluntly, "Unless you take change by the hand, it will take you by the throat."

As the old proverb goes, "The journey of a thousand miles begins with a single step." That step, if you've got the courage, could be calling your managers together to say, "I need your help to come up with fresh ideas to improve employee morale." At that point, a recognition program may play a key role in your company's future.

"We wildly underestimate the POWER of the tiniest personal TOUCH." Tom Peters

make PEOPLE
Feel
important

*e*arly in her career, Mary Kay Ash, the founder of Mary Kay Cosmetics, had been with a certain company for a short time, and was attending her first national convention. She was excited and wanted to learn all she could to achieve success in her new career. Suddenly, she saw him: the sales legend who had been #1 for years. She made her way through the crowd, and when she finally got the opportunity to speak, she asked for his advice. He turned and walked away as if she didn't exist.

In some ways, this was a defining moment in Mary Kay's life. She promised herself that if she were to ever have the opportunity to lead and share her knowledge with others, she would. Throughout her career, this quality has been her trademark, and has endeared her to all her employees. She loves people, and has said, "Whenever I meet someone I pretend they have a large sign around their neck that says 'Make Me Feel Important.'"

All human beings have the need to feel important and recognition is a key way we can meet that need. Making people feel important is the key to understanding recognition. There are no exceptions.

"There are TWO things people want more than sex and money. Recognition and praise." Mary Kay Ash

Establish "PEOPLE" goals

People goals should be articulated and defined so that they complement the other goals of the company. Morale, productivity and customer service are all related, and all can be impacted by the way a company does, or does not, recognize the people involved. Like any goal statement, a good recognition goal ought to be simple to understand and should satisfy the following criteria.

- Achievable: The most effective and motivating goals are those that people believe they can achieve if they plan and execute properly.

- Specific: Improving morale is a great idea, but it is too general. Specific definition on the action steps will help translate ideas into real progress.

- Measurable: To be effective, any goal must be measurable. If it cannot be evaluated objectively, then the employee will believe that only luck or personality will lead to success.

Finally, goals should be stated in specific time frames. Quantifiable tracking of activities deserving recognition for safety (reduction of accidents), quality (number of defects), customer satisfaction (number of calls/returns), or any other area which is directly impacted by employee appreciation will strengthen the integrity and commitment of everyone involved.

"It's not great ideas that SUCCEED, it's great people who make them succeed."

INVOLVE all your employees

there is little value in having a program where only a few employees have the opportunity to be recognized. When implemented correctly, there is not a department or position that cannot be included.

Everyone, no matter what their position, does contribute, and usually has the capacity to contribute more. The pivotal factor is finding ways to involve them.

Involving employees in decisions and opening up to their suggestions costs little but delivers big returns. Data from the Employee Involvement Association suggests that more than 6000 companies now have some formal involvement program, and that employee suggestions contribute savings in excess of two billion dollars each year. For every 100 employees eligible to participate, the annual savings are approximately $50,000. (That's almost $500 per eligible employee per year!)

Needless to say, it pays to acknowledge employee suggestions and to recognize them on a regular basis. In addition to the savings realized by implementing the ideas, there is also much to be gained by the improved communication. The process of listening sincerely and acknowledging employee suggestions may seem like a little thing, but the difference it makes can be tremendous.

"Empower the PEOPLE around you to win, and they will make you a winner." Michelle Weir

IDENTIFY the
recognition
CHAMPION

*a*lmost everyone wants to go to heaven. They just don't want to die to get there. Likewise, most managers feel that employee recognition is important, but they rarely find the time to do anything about it.

Think about the message this is sending. We're too busy with meetings, reports, and daily crises to focus on what is the most important asset of any company . . . its people.

For these reasons, I recommend a "Recognition Champion" be appointed by the CEO. This can be part of other job responsibilities, but should be an important part. It is the Champion's responsibility to assist, educate, and remind managers to keep the fire alive; to make recognition a part of their daily lives. This "point person" should coordinate meetings, purchase awards, answer questions, and, if necessary, prod managers. The Champion also meets monthly with the CEO to offer an on-going assessment of the mission.

Since people skills are critical, the Recognition Champion should ideally come from either customer service or human resources. They should be energetic, service oriented and respected by their peers. They should also be excited about the new challenge and believe in the power of recognition.

"BELIEF fuels passion
and PASSION rarely fails."

Managers will MAKE IT or BREAK IT

One person does not a recognition culture make. Ideally, support for any recognition program starts at the top. However, the key to its success are the managers of each department. Their attitude, and their commitment to making it all it can be is paramount.

According to author Carl Mays, a recent study of 25,000 employees in a wide range of companies found that 69% of their job satisfaction is derived from a manager's leadership skills. The study concluded that a good manager believes in employee recognition, and practices it on a daily basis by providing:

• A sense of mission.
• Support in developing abilities.
• Recognition of performance.
• An opportunity to share ideas.
• An opportunity to grow.

"If you plant CRAB APPLES don't count on harvesting golden delicious." Bill Meyer

always EXPRESS
Appreciation

So, you want a recognition program for your company. Now the question is what to do to thank people for a job well done. Well, all organizations are different. One may decide to send handwritten "thank you" notes and another may decide to pay a $20,000 cash bonus. The key is to be sincere, fair, and consistent. One or more of the suggestions below may make an employee feel like a hero. Remember, we all want recognition; we all want to feel important. Your job as a manager is to make recognition moments memorable. You have the opportunity to create some of those moments for your people. Don't waste it!

• Handwritten thank you notes from the president or manager.

• Public praise in a company or department meeting.

• Personalized awards or certificates to hang on a wall, or place on a desk.

• Cash awards, time off from work, tickets to athletic events, or dinner for two at a fine dining restaurant.

• Travel for two (either a weekend trip or an exciting destination for a week, depending on the achievement).

"We talk a lot about numbers. But our business is about PEOPLE. And by taking care of them, and our CUSTOMERS, the rest will come." Larry Stone

don't sweat
the small stuff,
just get the
DETAILS right

as a rule, good things happen when planned. Bad things happen on their own. So don't ignore an opportunity to map out a detailed plan with your managers, or to gather input from your employees. As Steven Covey says, "Start with the end in sight." If creating a recognition culture is your goal, then many hours of planning and follow-up need to happen.

• Create a Recognition Mission Statement with your managers, including criteria needed for certain ongoing awards (i.e. Employee of the Month, Sales Achievement, etc.).

• Develop timetables to make recognition announcements. Consistency is crucial to show your commitment and to establish the program's credibility with employees.

• Generate specific schedules for company and department meetings where exciting, memorable presentation makes it clear that recognition is a priority, not an afterthought.

• Develop a recognition report card to let the managers know how they're doing. Remember…old habits are not easily changed.

• Communicate, Communicate, Communicate. But never forget… it's not what you say, it's what they hear that counts.

"I can live a MONTH on a GOOD compliment." Mark Twain

don't EXPECT
PERFECTION

recognition is an art, not a science. Perfection is not an option. While planning is critical to developing a recognition culture, we must never forget it can ultimately only be measured in the attitudes of our employees (which translates to more satisfied customers.) Two reasons given by managers for not implementing recognition programs are:

• I'm not sure how to do it, and I don't want to make a mistake.

• I'm not sure the investment will generate a measurable return.

Both are reasonable concerns. However, if you believe, as Dr. Maslow does, that recognition and feeling important are basic human needs that drive behavior, then a leap of faith may be necessary. If you don't believe this, the nearest garbage can would be the best place for this book because nothing else will matter.

"I don't know the KEY to success, but the key to failure is trying to please everybody." Bill Cosby

Celebrate
SUCCESS

recognition is the art of making people feel important. Ongoing award programs that are consistently maintained, such as "Employee of the Month" awards for the company or department, can be extremely effective. Focus on the areas that fit your needs and you'll create a recognition culture that will make your company a great place to work.

- Establish an "Extra Mile" award for extraordinary effort, a "Team Player" award recognizing an unselfish spirit, or "Customer Service" awards, which can be awarded for individual acts of service or for an employee's outstanding attitude.

- Create sales awards for the day, the week, or the month.

- Start a "Rookie of the Year" award, presented to a new employee who has the best attitude or who has made a great contribution to sales or profits.

- Initiate productivity awards to celebrate contributions in manufacturing, warehouse and shipping environments.

- Don't forget service awards to recognize key employee anniversaries such as 1, 5 and 10 years, as well as safety awards tied to employee accident records, and awards for outstanding suggestions.

"People are like a storage battery, constantly discharging ENERGY, and UNLESS they are recharged at frequent intervals, they soon run dry."

change COMPANY

Culture

any time you mention the words "change" and "culture" in the same sentence, three more words automatically come to mind, "It ain't easy." But it can be done. Here are some tips to begin creating a recognition culture within your company.

- Start at the top. The CEO must be passionate about making recognition a priority.

- Sell your managers and get their input. Help them understand the relationship between satisfied customers and happy employees. Then ask – what can we do to improve employee morale through recognition?

- Involve your employees. When in doubt ask the people in question. Although you can never please all of the people all of the time, rest assured they'll appreciate you valuing their opinion.

- Appoint a recognition champion. This individual, appointed by the president, will work with managers to help insure the success of the program.

- Make it fun and memorable. Be creative to make sure you keep it fresh.

"We cannot go back and make a new start, but we can start new and make a NEW ENDING."

SET the
example

nothing can be more un-motivating than establishing specific, measurable goals for your employees and then failing to track their performance and acknowledge the achievement. If no feedback is given, then why should employees put forth the effort. It suggests that the goals are unimportant.

A poor example undermines credibility, and once compromised, it takes a long time to get it back. Set an example by following these guidelines.

- Acknowledge achievements as they happen. The sooner you reward progress, the greater the likelihood that the desired behavior will be repeated. Late recognition is weak recognition.

- Be consistent in prosperity and adversity. Many managers make the mistake of tying the need for recognition to their financial fortunes of the moment. Don't be one of them. To maintain credibility with your employees you must be consistent in good times and bad.

- Tie recognition results to manager's job performance. If a manager knows that job performance will be partially measured by how successfully their recognition program was implemented, you'll get their attention.

- Publicly communicate progress. Visually illustrating performance on significant issues in a way everyone can observe is a great way to promote teamwork and establish a shared commitment.

"Employees are like children.
Don't expect them to LISTEN to your advice
and to ignore your example." John Capozzi

CREATE
moments to
Remember

Sally Duncan has been selected as the April Employee of the Month for your company. Which of these scenarios do you feel will have a lasting impact?

Scenario 1: Sally's boss at a staff meeting stands up to say: "I'm pleased to say that Sally Duncan has been selected as our April Employee of the Month" (presents the award).

Scenario 2: The company president at a monthly meeting attended by all employees has this to say: "As I've grown older, I've come to realize it's not what people say, it's what they do that matters. Our April Employee of the Month is a doer. She's always got a smile on her face and she's always willing to help. She's a team player who consistently goes the extra mile to get the job done. Please stand up to congratulate Sally Duncan, our April Employee of the Month" (presents the award).

I think you get the picture. Research shows that the recipient's interaction with management and peers is more important than the award itself. In this case not only do you want to create a moment that Sally will remember forever, you also want other employees to understand why she is being recognized.

The lesson learned is to never underestimate the magic that combining the right words, in front of the right people will create. People cherish specific moments in their lives. You have a golden opportunity, don't waste it.

"Compensation is a RIGHT, recognition is a GIFT." Rosabeth M. Kanter

never
UNDERESTIMATE the
POWER
of Kindness

kindness, in my opinion, is the ultimate form of recognition. It honors human dignity, it sincerely listens to ideas of others, and it radiates compassion, love and respect. Kindness can be offered by anyone, in any company, in any home, or on any street corner. If each day, every person would perform one simple, unexpected act of kindness, the world would never be the same. Some simple ideas for the workplace include:

• Listening – you can convey no greater honor than to sincerely listen to what someone has to say.

• A heartfelt verbal thank you or congratulations.

• An unexpected voice mail or e-mail to show your appreciation.

• A handwritten note, birthday card or birthday message.

• A single rose on the desk of someone who went "above and beyond."

• "MAY I HELP?" are the three most appreciated words in the English language. Use them often.

"Kindness is a language we can all speak. Even the deaf can HEAR it and the BLIND can see." Mother Teresa

Don't Wait
for your SHIP TO
COME IN,
SWIM out
to it

The greatest teams are comprised of motivated and unselfish individuals. Your job as a manager is to build a great team and you know your success is tied to how well you can motivate each person to reach their full potential. You believe in the power of recognition and want to do more, but there is no formal support at the top. What do you do?

Act now. Go with your gut. Put your ideas into action! View it as an opportunity to blaze the recognition trail for your company. Your team will benefit, your company will benefit, and your career will benefit.

"Don't be afraid
TO GO OUT ON A LIMB; that's where
the fruit is."

Mac Anderson is the founder of Successories, Inc., the leader in designing and marketing products for business and personal motivation.

With 400 employees, the company mails more than 12 million catalogs a year, and operates 75 retail stores in malls around the country.

Prior to Successories, Anderson was also involved in two other successful startup companies. He was the founder of McCord Travel, which he sold to Helene Curtis in 1985. Today, McCord is the largest travel company in the Midwest with sales over $1 billion. He was also the Vice President of Sales and part owner of Orval Kent Food Company, where he received the Marketing Excellence Award from Sales and Marketing Magazine.

Anderson's ability to motivate himself throughout his entrepreneurial career stems from his passion. His philosophy in business and life has remained constant, "To love what you do, and feel that it matters, how could it be more fun."

In addition to *Companies Don't Succeed... People Do*, he is the author of *Motivating Yourself*; he also does keynote speeches for companies and associations on these topics.

To contact Anderson for a speaking engagement, call the Successories corporate headquarters in Aurora, Illinois, at 800-621-1423, or e-mail him at manderson@successories.com.

a single book could never lay out all the details of a recognition program that fits your specific needs. I'm happy if this book has simply convinced you that you need such a program, while outlining fundamentals that will ensure success. The details as how you structure, implement, and measure your own recognition program should evolve from discussions with your managers and employees. By sharing with you what has worked well for other companies, the following titles also offer valuable guidelines and suggestions.

- 1001 Ways to Reward Employees *by Bob Nelson* $10.95

- 1001 Ways to Energize Employees *by Bob Nelson* $10.95

- Getting Employees to Fall in Love with Your Company
  by Jim Harris $17.95

These books can be purchased at your local bookstore, or at any Successories retail store. For the location of the Successories store nearest you, call (800) 956-2286.

"A paycheck is what an employee
lives on. Recognition and
appreciation is what they live for."

The cost is low...
but the ideas are priceless!

Share these books with your entire organization and watch the power of your team grow!

Each title in the Successories "Power of One" library takes less than 30 minutes to read, but the wisdom they contain will last a lifetime. Take advantage of volume pricing as you share these insights with all the people who impact your career, your business and your life.

Anatomy of A Leader
Carl Mays
This body of knowledge can help everyone develop the qualities of a leader. #NF713259

Attitude: Your Internal Compass
Denis Waitley and Boyd Matheson
These practical insights will help managers and employees maintain a positive outlook each day. #NF713193

Burn Brightly Without Burning Out
Dick Biggs
Boost morale and productivity by helping people balance the work they do with the life they lead. #NF716016

Companies Don't Succeed... People Do
Mac Anderson
Learn to develop employees and a recognition culture within any organization. #NF716015

Dare to Soar
Byrd Baggett
The spirit of eagles inspired this unique collection of motivational thoughts. #NF716006

The Employee Connection
Jim Harris
Learn to empower your people through open communication with these valuable tips. #NF716018

Empowerment
Ken Blanchard and Susan Fowler Woodring
Use these valuable ideas to achieve "Peak Performance Through Self-Leadership." #NF716022

Fall In Love with Your Future
Ron and Mary Beshear
Apply the principles outlined in this refreshing book and begin to take control of your future. #NF716026

Goals
Gary Ryan Blair
A refreshing mix of insights and thought-provoking exercises make this a "Guideline for Designing an Extraordinary Life." #NF716025

Ignite Your Creative Spark
Jordan Ayan
This book will reveal your hidden potential as it inspires new vistas of creative exploration. #NF716023

Motivating Today's Employees
Bob Nelson
Use this book to understand the impact of employee rewards and recognition. #NF716007

Motivating Yourself
Mac Anderson
This unique mix of proven ideas and motivating stories will help "Recharge the Human Battery." #NF716021

Motivation, Lombardi Style
Vince Lombardi
Inspire your team with these insights about the athletic playing field and the business battlefield. #NF716013

Priorities
Peggy Anderson
Learn about what it takes to "Make a Difference in the Life of a Child" and share it with others. #NF716027

The Psychology of Winning for the 21st Century
Dr. Denis Waitley
Dr. Denis Waitley provides a unique perspective on what it means to win in the 21st Century. #NF716024

Pulling Together
John Murphy
Share "The 17 Principles of Effective Teamwork" with every member of any team. #NF716019

Quality, Service, Teamwork
This valuable resource includes over 100 motivational quotes on various topics. #NF716014

Results
Jeff Blackman
Help your sales team turn passion into profit with these "Proven Strategies for Changing Times." #NF716017

Rule #One
C. Leslie Charles
There are common sense tips and easy-to-apply rules in this customer service handbook. #NF716008

Teamwork
Glenn Parker
This is a valuable blueprint for successful team building. Put it to work for your team. #NF716012

Think Change
John Murphy
This provocative commentary is designed to change people's thinking—"To Adapt and Thrive or Fall Behind." #NF716020

We've Got to Start Meeting Like This
Ron Fry
Learn to reach for results and get more out of your team meetings with these insightful tips. #NF716028

Everything You Need to Know to Get Everything You Want
Robert Stuberg
Your view of yourself and the world around you will change as you discover and apply these "Life Secrets for Success." #NF716029

Heartpower
Jim Harris, Ph.D.
This valuable advice is intended to "Get Your People to Love Your Company." #NF716030